Travel Through Time
Riding the Rails

Rail Travel Past and Present

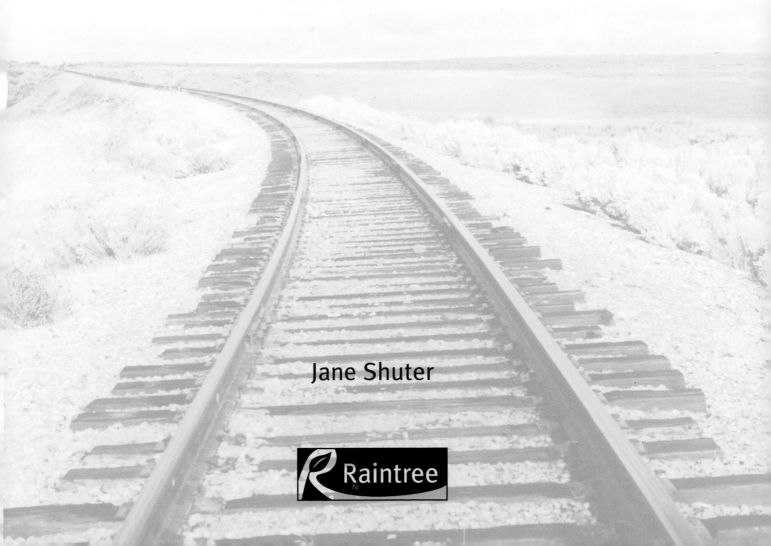

Jane Shuter

Raintree

www.raintreepublishers.co.uk
Visit our website to find out more information about **Raintree** books.

To order:
☎ Phone 44 (0) 1865 888112
📄 Send a fax to 44 (0) 1865 314091
💻 Visit the Raintree Bookshop at **www.raintreepublishers.co.uk** to browse our catalogue and order online.

First published in Great Britain by Raintree, Halley Court, Jordan Hill, Oxford OX2 8EJ, part of Harcourt Education.
Raintree is a registered trademark of Harcourt Education Ltd.

Editorial: Nick Hunter and Catherine Clarke
Design: Michelle Lisseter and Bigtop
Picture Research: Maria Joannou and Kathryn Kollberg
Production: Jonathan Smith

Originated by Dot Gradations Ltd
Printed and bound in China by South China Printing Company

ISBN 1 844 43505 9
08 07 06 05 04
10 9 8 7 6 5 4 3 2 1

British Library Cataloguing in Publication Data
Shuter, Jane
Riding the Rails: rail travel past and present–
(Travel Through Time)
385'.09
A full catalogue record for this book is available from the British Library.

Acknowledgements
The publishers would like to thank the following for permission to reproduce photographs:
AKG p. **13**; Bridgeman Art Library pp. **4** (The Stapleton Collection), **7** (Hatton Gallery, University of Newcastle), **8** (Science Museum), **11**, **12** (Private collection); Corbis pp. **10**, **17** (E. J. Frazier), **21** (Randy Faris), **29** (Hashimoto Noboru); Hulton Archive pp. **14**, **18**; John Seely p. **6**; London Transport Museum p. **20**; Mary Evans Picture Library pp. **9**, **16** (Library of Congress), **25**; Milepost p. **28**; Peter Newark's Military Photos p. **15**; Popperfoto pp. **19**, **26**; QA Photo Library pp. **23**; Rail Images pp. **5**, **27**; Robert Harding Picture Library p. **22**; Science Photo Library p. **24**.

Cover photograph of a railroad poster reproduced with permission of Corbis.

Every effort has been made to contact copyright holders of any material reproduced in this book. Any omissions will be rectified in subsequent printings if notice is given to the publishers.

The paper used to print this book comes from sustainable resources.

Contents

Any words appearing in bold, **like this**, are explained in the Glossary.

Travel by rail

People began to travel on railways in the 1800s. Before that, rails had been used to carry **goods** short distances. From the start, railways had a huge effect on people and places. People could travel further than they ever had before. They could go on day trips to a nearby city or seaside town. They could travel further to work on **commuter** trains. Trains even changed what people ate, as fresh food could be taken to markets further away.

HOW FAST?

London to Liverpool (346 kilometres, or 215 miles)

Year	Vehicle	Time of journey
1836	coach	21 hrs 15 minutes
1844	train	8 hrs 15 minutes
1900	train	4 hrs 15 minutes
1914	train	3 hrs 35 minutes
2000	train	3 hrs 35 minutes.

This engraving from 1839 shows a steam train leaving its engine house.

4

Changing the land

Railways made other changes, too. In hilly country, workers had to dig tunnels and **embankments**, and build bridges over rivers and **canals**. So the land looked different once the railways came. In the USA the railways travelled right across the country, from the east coast to the west coast.

Workers needed!

Thousands of workers were needed to build the railways, and to work on them once they were built.

08:23·57

3

In today's cities, many people need trains to take them to work or school each day.

Early railways

People disagree about who built the earliest railways.

The ancient Greeks?

The ancient Greeks used ruts carved in a stone path to haul ships across a strip of land from the Aegean Sea to the Ionian Sea. Some people say this is an early railway because trucks ran along a fixed track carrying something (ships). Other people say this was not a railway because the trucks ran in grooves, not on rails.

These ancient paving stones in Pompeii had wheel ruts, or grooves, so that vehicles could travel down them more smoothly.

Wooden rails

The first vehicles to use rails ran on wooden rails. We do not know exactly when people began using wooden rails. People have written about wooden railways since the 1600s. The oldest wooden railway that has survived to the present was built in the north of England. It moved coal from the bottom to the top of a mine.

HEAVY LOADS

The first railways were useful for pulling heavy loads, because they did not get stuck in mud or ruts as road vehicles did. However, railways were slower than the horse-drawn vehicles on the road.

This painting from the 1800s shows a railway being used in a coal mine.

Iron rails and steam

Before the 1790s all vehicles had to be pulled by people or animals. In the 1780s James Watt made a steam engine. The steam – made by burning coal and heating water – powered the movement. All through the 1790s **inventors**, especially in Britain and the USA, worked to make a steam engine to pull heavy loads and replace horsepower.

In 1808 an engineer in London showed off his engine, which could travel at 10 miles per hour, to crowds of people.

GEORGE STEPHENSON

George Stephenson, born in England in 1781, is called 'the father of the railways'. He built his first steam engine in 1814. He was employed to build the Stockton to Darlington railway in 1825. He worked on many railway projects until his death in 1848.

From coal to people

The Stockton to Darlington railway was built in 1825 to move **goods**. Soon it was carrying passengers, too. The next railway, from Liverpool to Manchester, was meant for passengers from the start. George Stephenson built it. He won a competition, the Rainhill Trials, because his engine, *Rocket*, was fastest. So, his engine was used on the new railway.

On the Stockton to Darlington railway the engine went 24 kilometres (15 miles) per hour. Coaches travelled at about 16 kilometres (10 miles) per hour at this time.

Further and faster

In 1830 the first US locomotive, *Best Friend of Charleston* ran a 9.5 kilometre (6 mile) route from Charleston to a nearby town. In 1831 it reached a speed of 40 kilometres (25 miles) per hour.

Early train travel

Many people were against the railways in the 1830s and 1840s. Coach and **canal** companies feared the railways would take their customers. Many ordinary people were also against the railways. They said trains went too fast and that the sparks from the burning coal, which made the steam, might easily set light to things. Also, farmers said the noise would scare their animals.

No stopping them

Despite the objections, railways were built very quickly. They proved to be quick, **convenient** and popular. In 1830 Britain had 129 kilometres (80 miles) of track, by 1850 it was about 10,000 kilometres (6200 miles).

This is one of the earliest US trains.

This train has hard wooden seats. The sides are open to the weather and smoke from the engine.

SPEED!

The speed of rail travel made up for the discomfort. A lady travelling in 1836 said: 'The 36 miles [58 kilometres] took an hour and a half. By coach it is over four hours. It is smoother than a coach and the speed is not alarming, because it is steady'.

Early train travel was uncomfortable. The coal burned to make the steam caused most of the problems. The smoke smelt bad and made eyes water. The **smuts** made clothes dirty and the sparks could burn.

Building a railway

Building a railway was a big, expensive job. First, railway **engineers** had to decide where to build it. Most railways joined two big towns, with stops along the way. Then they had to buy, or get permission to build on, the land. Some landowners did not want the railway crossing their land. So not all railways go in a straight line!

Building work

Railways needed to run flat, not go up or down steep hills. So engineers had to dig **cuttings** or tunnels through hills and build bridges across rivers and **canals**.

Hard rock had to be blasted out of the way with explosives to make tunnels and cuttings.

A dangerous job

Building a railway needed thousands of workers. They were badly paid to do a dangerous job. One doctor in England worked with the **navvies** on the line from Sheffield to Manchester. In the six years it took to build, there were 'hundreds' of deaths. He treated nearly 700 injuries.

NAVVIES

The workers who built the railways were often called navvies, short for 'navigators'. They lived and worked in terrible conditions. They had camps with no clean water or toilets. The work, especially digging tunnels, was dangerous and unhealthy.

Navvies often came from poor **immigrant** groups.

Railway mania

By the end of 1850 Britain had around 10,000 kilometres (6200 miles) of track. Different companies built different lines of different widths. Train timetables did not work together, so long journeys were difficult.

What's the time?

In 1800, time varied across Britain by as much as half an hour, depending on when the sun rose and set. The railways meant time had to be made the same all over the country, or timetables would not work.

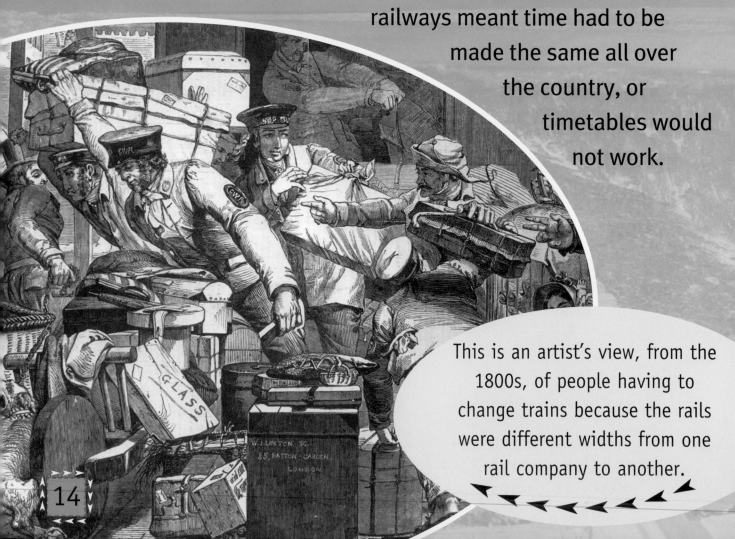

This is an artist's view, from the 1800s, of people having to change trains because the rails were different widths from one rail company to another.

Railways in Europe

Some countries took to railways quickly. King Leopold of Belgium wanted a national rail **network**. He planned it and employed British **engineers** and workmen to build it. He ended up with a better system than Britain! The King of Spain refused to have railways built at all.

FIRST PASSENGER RAILWAYS

Country	First passenger railway
UK	1825
USA	1830
France	1832
Belgium	1835
Australia	1854

Railways were very important in the development of the West in the USA.

Crossing a continent

Before the railways

Railways made a huge difference to big countries such as the USA. Before the railways, crossing the USA took many months. If travellers got lost, or mistimed their journey, they could get injured or die, in the baking heat or freezing snow.

The rails of the US Central Pacific and Union Pacific met near Great Salt Lake, Utah.

Railways

Railways were quickly laid all over the USA. In 1869 the Central Pacific and Union Pacific railways met near Great Salt Lake, Utah. When they joined, there was a railway 2858 kilometres (1776 miles) across the USA.

Some accidents happened because lines froze in cold weather.

KEEPING CALM

Because of the long distances involved, passengers sometimes had to wait a long time for help to arrive if their train broke down. When a train hit some cows in Nevada in the 1850s the driver went for help. The passengers had to cut up and eat some cows to survive until they were rescued.

The railways made crossing the USA safer, but it was not entirely safe. Trains often broke down, or ran out of fuel, leaving passengers stranded. Sometimes, trains hit animals on the line and broke down. Engine drivers had to make clever repairs or difficult journeys for help. They became heroes.

Difficult railways

The Trans-Siberian Railway

The Trans-Siberian Railway was begun in 1891. It was not finished until 1904. It stretched 9198 kilometres (5778 miles) right across Russia and had over 1000 stations. Criminals were used to build the worst section. They had to work in temperatures of -22° Celsius.

These Russian criminals were used to build part of the Siberian Railway.

Across the desert

The workers who built the railways in Australia faced very different problems from those who built the Trans-Siberian Railway. They had to cope with scorching hot weather, because a third of Australia is desert.

AUSTRALIA'S RAILWAYS

Australia began as six separate colonies. They each built their own stretches of railway. Like the early railways in Britain, these railways had different widths of rail. Between 1911 and 1917 workers built a 1691-kilometre (1051-mile) railway right across the country.

This Austrian train is going up a steep hill. It would slip on ordinary rails, so the tracks have 'teeth' like a zip.

Underground railways

Railways usually joined one big town to another. People in big cities wanted to use railways to get around, but cities were crammed with buildings. Too many buildings would have to be knocked down to build a useful system of railways around the city.

The London Underground system grew very quickly. Charing Cross station is shown photographed here in 1894.

Engineers decided to use the tunnelling skills of their workers to build whole railway systems under the buildings. The world's first underground system was built in London. The first line, the Metropolitan Line, opened in 1863.

Travelling underground

Early underground travel was unpleasant. The first passengers travelled in open carriages and the trains were steam-powered. So the dark tunnels held all the smoke, **smuts** and sparks in. It was not until 1890 that the London Underground started using electric engines.

Elevated railways, first laid out in the 1890s are still in use today.

GOING OVER

In some cities, such as Chicago, USA, **elevated** rail lines were built over the roads and between the buildings. In some ways this was easier than tunnelling underground. The Chicago Loop system was finished in 1897 and is still running. It carries over 220 million passengers a year.

Undergrounds everywhere

From London, undergrounds spread worldwide. In the USA, Boston opened a **subway** (the US word for underground railway) in 1897. In 1904, New York opened its first subway.

THE WORLD'S UNDERGROUNDS

1897 Boston, USA
1900 Paris, France
1919 Madrid, Spain
1927 Tokyo, Japan
1935 Moscow, Russia

Playing sardines?

Many city undergrounds set up in the late 1800s or early 1900s are still used. They are extended, repaired and kept running. The cities have grown and the undergrounds have to carry far more passengers. At busy times they get very overcrowded.

In Tokyo rush hours, station workers push passengers into trains.

The drill used on the Channel Tunnel was enormous compared to an ordinary electric drill.

A BIG TUNNEL

In 1994 the Channel Tunnel opened, under the sea between England and France. It was built using the tunnelling technology used in underground building. It stretches for 49.9 kilometres (31 miles) and carries cars and lorries, on special trains.

People are still building and extending underground systems. They are still one of the best ways to get around a city. The Moscow metro has the longest single underground tunnel. It is 37.8 kilometres (23.5 miles) long.

New fuels

All early trains, overground or underground, were powered by steam engines. The steam was made by burning coal to boil water. Steam engines took time to build up steam. It was also difficult to keep the steam pressure steady. People wanted to find new fuels.

Petrol to diesel

When the petrol engine was used in cars, it was tried in trains. Petrol trains were too dangerous, though, and needed to re-fuel often. In 1892 Rudolf Diesel invented the diesel engine. Diesel trains used less fuel and were safer.

This early electric passenger railway was first shown to the public in Berlin in 1879.

Electric trains

Thomas Davenport, an American, **invented** the electric train in the 1800s. However, the first electric train service did not run until 1881, in Germany. In the USA in 1895 the Baltimore and Ohio Railroad started using electric trains. They spread all over the world, because different fuels can be used to make electricity, so countries can use whatever fuel is cheapest there.

MONORAILS

Monorail trains run on one rail; either on top of it, or underneath it. The first one was used in 1825. Monorails are less stable than a train on two rails, so cannot go as fast – but they are cheaper and cleaner.

LISTOWEL & BALLYBUNION RLY. ENGINE.

This monorail train was painted in the 1890s.

Controlling trains

Early trains were controlled very simply. The driver leaned out of the train to look for problems on the line. Men along the line signalled trains to stop or go. The only other controls were **points** to switch rails when lines divided. Someone stood by the line when trains were due and switched the points by hand.

Too fast

As trains went faster, it became harder to see the signaller. Mechanical **signals**, worked from a signal box, were **invented**.

Each handle works a different signal. The railway worker has to remember what each numbered handle means.

More trains

More trains meant more track, more points to change and more chances of accidents. The invention of electricity meant people could use a system of lights, like road traffic lights, to control trains. These lights work together, changing when the train has passed them.

KEEPING TRACK

Now people can use computers to see where trains are on their tracks. They can also change points and signals automatically, although they still need people to mend the track or fix jammed points. They can get in touch with the driver if there is a problem.

Modern railways

Railways are still important for carrying **goods** and for getting people around in cities. People are working hard on different kinds of power and rails to make trains go faster. They have to be faster, to compete with aeroplanes.

This japanese bullet train is one of the fastest in the world.

The 'bullet train'

The Japanese began to run their high-speed train, the 'bullet train', in 1964. The train can reach a speed of 443 kilometres (275 miles) per hour, but only runs with passengers at a top speed of 299 kilometres (186 miles) per hour.

TGV

The French high-speed train *Train à Grand Vitesse* (**TGV** for short) first ran in 1981. Its top speed with passengers is usually 249 kilometres (155 miles) per hour, although it can go as fast as 515 kilometres (320 miles) per hour.

The Maglev train in China can reach up to 500 kilometres (311 miles) per hour.

THE LATEST THING

The Shanghai Maglev (*magnetic levitation*) train made its first trip on 1 January 2003. **Magnetic levitation trains** use powerful magnets to 'float' the trains above the track. The Shanghai train did a 31-kilometre (19-mile) trip to the city airport in 8 minutes. The trip takes 45 minutes by road.

Find out for yourself

You can find out more about the history of rail travel by talking to older people about how travel has changed during their lifetimes. Your local library will have books about this. They may have newspapers and magazine articles from the time, as well. You will find the answers to many of your questions in this book, but you can also use other books and the Internet.

Books to read

I Didn't Know That: Some Trains Run On Water and other amazing facts about rail transport, Kate Petty (Millbrook Press, 1997)
Take-off! Transport Around the World: Trains, Chris Oxlade (Heinemann Library, 2002)

Using the Internet

Explore the Internet to find out more about rail travel. Websites can change, but if the link below no longer works, don't worry. Use a search engine, such as www.yahooligans.com or www.internet4kids.com, and type in keywords such as 'railways', '**elevated** railways', 'underground railways' (or '**subways**') and particular famous routes, such as 'Trans-Siberian Railway'.

Websites

www.trakkies.co.uk/historyzone/first.html
This site contains lots of pictures and is full of facts on trains and important **inventors**.

Disclaimer
All the Internet addresses (URLs) given in this book were valid at the time of going to press. However, due to the dynamic nature of the Internet, some addresses may have changed, or sites may have ceased to exist since publication. While the author and publishers regret any inconvenience this may cause readers, no responsibility for any such changes can be accepted by either the author or the publishers.

Glossary

canal waterway made by people

commuter person who travels quite a long distance from home to work each day

convenient easy

cutting path for a road or railway line that is cut out of a hill to keep it flat, rather than running over the hill

elevated something raised up above ground level

embankment steep sides of a railway, in between which the train runs on rails

engineer person who works out how to build something, like a railway, road or bridge, so that it works and is safe

goods things that are made, bought and sold

immigrant person who comes to live in a foreign country

invent make or discover something for the first time

magnetic levitation train train that moves along a rail powered by magnets pushing away from each other

monorail train that runs on a single rail (under or over the train) instead of a rail on each side of the train

navvies men who worked on the building of railways

network a rail network is lots of different lines that all link up

points switches used where one line splits and goes off in two or more directions

signal something that can be seen from a long way off, to give a warning

smuts bits of burnt coal that are carried in the air by wind

subway underground train service, or a passage for people to cross busy roads by going under them

TGV fast French train, called TGV from the first letters of the French *train à grand vitesse*, which means 'very fast train'

Index